THE

COMING

An Advent Devotional by Becca Harbert

BexBooks

Indianapolis

To Barb Wiles, the biggest encourager for my writing.

To my former small group ladies: Lauren, Erin, Elise, Kyndall, and Lilly. For showing me the need for women to see modern day applications to the ancient Biblical text.

The Coming King: An Advent Devotional

By Becca Harbert

Edited by Deb Davis

BexBooks Publishing, Indianapolis By Becca Harbert Library of Congress Control Number: ##### ISBN 978-1-943831-06-7 Published in 2024 by BexBooks Text copyright © 2024 by Becca Harbert. Printed in the United States of America. Scripture taken from the Holy Bible, New Living Translation, copyright © 1996, 2004, 2015 by Tyndale House Foundation. Used by permission of Tyndale House Publishers, Inc., Carol Stream, Illinois 60188. All rights reserved.

Table of Contents

Introduction

Hello Friend!

This book is written for YOU! Another year. Another
Advent. Another time of trying to prepare our hearts and
minds for the birth of Christ. How do we make it meaningful
again, in a fresh new light? Let me remind you, as John
MacArthur once said, simply reminding each other of the
truths of God's Word is enough. It doesn't always have to feel
fresh, new, super-light-bulb-aha-moment. It can be subtle
reminders of truths learned long ago that we reflect on in new
seasons of life. While I do hope you learn from this Advent
devotional, I also know all too well the pressure to make
Christmas special, better, more about Christ, more restful,
more social, more everything. I pray you find this devotional
to be both a blessing and an anchor, reminding you of the
reason for the season. I pray this better enables you to keep
your eyes fixed on Jesus in the midst of whatever you face this
season.

1
The Messiah Will Reconcile

"And I will cause hostility between you and the woman, and between your offspring and her offspring. He will strike your head, and you will strike his heel" (Genesis 3:15).
"But when the right time came, God sent his Son, born of a woman, subject to the law. God sent him to buy freedom for us who were slaves to the law, so that he could adopt us as his very own children" (Galatians 4:4-5).

In a fight between two men, where one had his Achilles tendon cut and the other received a baseball bat to his head, who would win? Personally, I think the one with the head injury would lose. After Adam and Eve ate the forbidden fruit, God said Jesus would strike the serpent's head, but the serpent would strike Jesus' heel (Genesis 3:15). In other words, the devil may have won that battle, but Jesus would win the war!

God, in His loving mercy, had a plan, even when His created humans ruined His original design. God did not sit around wondering what to do next after Adam and Eve ate the forbidden fruit. God did not anxiously try to figure out plan B. God also did not react in anger toward those who had disobeyed Him. Instead, He calmly said, "Ok, here's what's going to happen now as a result. It will be difficult for a while, and I tried to shelter you from that, but I have a plan that will eventually ease your pain." The devil's plan to ruin redemption for the world was ruined by Jesus' perfect life, sinless death, and resurrection.

Christmas is very much a celebration of a reconciled relationship between God and humankind. That rekindling of relationships, through Christmas cards, parties, and reunions, is not too far off from God's original intent for Christmas. Without Adam and Eve's big mistake, we would not have this beautiful thing called Christmas. We would not have a need for it. Through an enormous mistake came an even bigger solution: the greatest act of love, the final act of reconciliation.

This Christmas season, take opportunities to reconnect relationally with others as gifts from God. If you find yourself dealing with a big mistake (yours or someone else's), remember that God is not anxiously wondering what to do next. He always still has a plan for you. His mercies are still new, every morning (Lamentations 3:22-23). If He can redeem all of mankind after Adam and Eve ruined it, He can surely redeem the things in your life. His plan of redemption was not thwarted when Adam and Eve sinned. Neither is His plan for you.

The Messiah Will Be Born of a Virgin

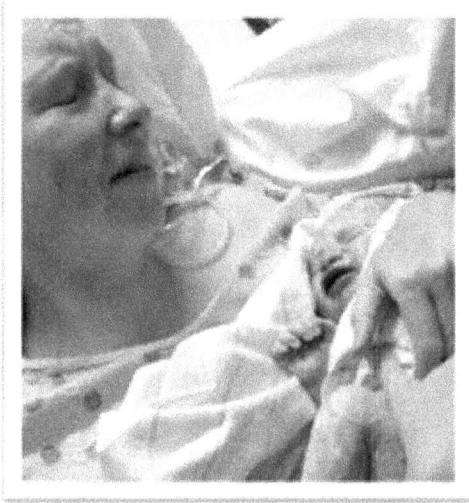

*"All right then, the Lord himself will give you the sign.
Look! The virgin will conceive a child! She will give birth to
a son and will call him Immanuel (which means 'God is with
us')" (Isaiah 7:14).*
*"Mary asked the angel, 'But how can this happen? I am a
virgin.' The angel replied, 'The Holy Spirit will come upon
you, and the power of the Most High will overshadow you.
So the baby to be born will be holy, and he will be called the
Son of God'" (Luke 1:34-35).*

I had to be induced a week after my due date with one
of my children because even after my water broke, I was not
in labor. After a few hours of not much progress, all of a
sudden, the baby wanted out ASAP! That child went from
wanting to stay put to coming out so quickly! That very much
describes his personality today. He cannot be pushed to do
anything. But once he sets his mind to do something, nothing

can stop him. I share that because I learned something about my child's personality from his birth story.

What do we learn about Jesus from His birth story? Our verse says "the virgin will conceive" (Isaiah 7:14). Every baby is a miracle, but some more than others, and Jesus most of all. We get so used to the idea of Jesus being "born of a virgin," that we forget the miraculous-ness of it. Born of a virgin! Can you imagine the absurdity of it? That had *never* happened before, nor again! What about artificial insemination, you ask? Well, yes, in a spiritual sense, that's what the Holy Spirit did. He artificially, supernaturally inseminated Mary in order to impregnate her with Jesus, your Savior. Is that TMI? Sorry! Being born of a virgin was not natural. It was *supernatural!* A supernatural birth means a supernatural Jesus. We also learn from His birth that Jesus' birth daddy was God, but His earthly father was Joseph. He's the Son of God. Lastly, through His birth, God proclaimed His purpose and plan for Jesus. Immanuel means "God with us." Because of Jesus, we are reconciled into a relationship *with* God.

As you celebrate Jesus' supernatural birth this year, consider your own. What does your earthly or even spiritual birth reveal about God's purpose for you? He has a purpose for you, and it's good. You may not have been born of a virgin, but you were still created miraculously by God and adopted into His family. He is still your heavenly Father and was present at your birth. Praise God, knowing that just as He had plans for you in your birth, He has plans for you today too. Amen!

The Messiah Will Be Called...

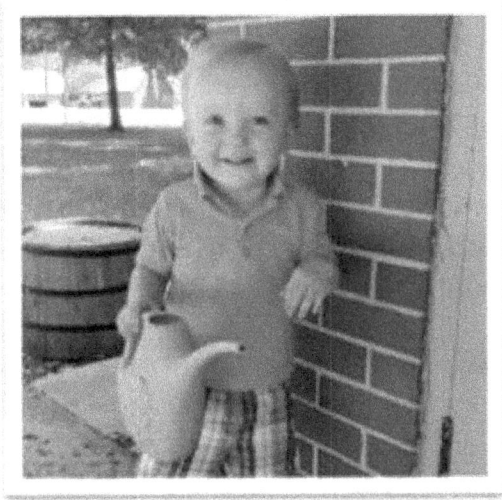

"For a child is born to us, a son is given to us. The government will rest on his shoulders. And he will be called: Wonderful Counselor, Mighty God, Everlasting Father, Prince of Peace" (Isaiah 9:6).
"He will be very great and will be called the Son of the Most High. The Lord God will give him the throne of his ancestor David" (Luke 1:32).

Imagine the hope a child brings, even in the midst of sorrow. Isaiah spoke to a people who felt forgotten by the Lord as their government crumbled. The Luke passage says the "throne of His ancestor David," referring to Jesus being a descendant of David and His reign being everlasting (Luke 1:32). Israel *always* had a descendant of David on the throne. Be encouraged as you reflect on the following titles for Christ.
Wonderful Counselor: We have all received bad advice at some point, but the prophesied One gives good advice and is

a good listener. Do you talk and pray to Jesus as if He can handle all your problems? I pray you allow Him to guide all your Christmas decisions. Aren't there oh so many?

Mighty God: Those feeling powerless under an oppressive government during Isaiah's time would have found great comfort in hearing about the mightiness of God. What news to hear about a God who loves them *and* cares about them *and* is able to *do* something about their situation! Do you see Him as mighty enough to fix a broken world? To fix your broken heart? I pray you look to Him as your mighty God, able to answer your deepest longings, more than even Santa. And if you are feeling OK, pray about who you can help carry a heavy load this season.

Everlasting Father: I always think of God the Father and Jesus the Son. But since Jesus is also God, He is also the everlasting Father. Confused yet? There are some spiritual truths our human minds will not comprehend until we enter Heaven. Jesus is the perfect Father who will never die. Well, not again anyway. Do you view Him as such, as the true Father of Christmas, delivering good gifts every day of the year?

Prince of Peace: In an oppressive regime, peace seems unattainable. The Prince of Peace can achieve what no one else can: true peace. Is there an area of your life where you feel animosity or tension that needs the peace of God? Let Jesus be your prince of Peace, calming you amidst the craziness of holiday traffic, crowds, and the pressure to do all the things perfectly.

4
The Messiah Will Be Born in Bethlehem

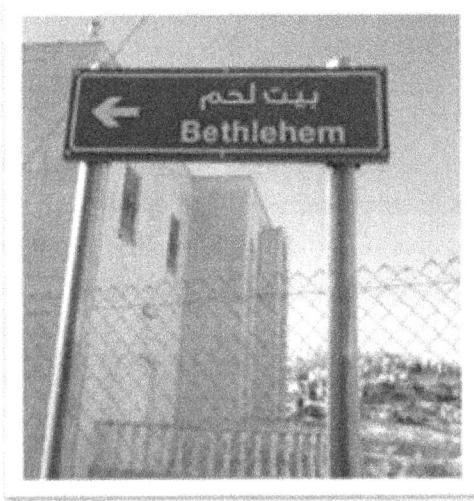

بيت لحم
Bethlehem

PC:
Mandy
Wiles

"But you, O Bethlehem Ephrathah, are only a small village among all the people of Judah. Yet a ruler of Israel, whose origins are in the distant past, will come from you on my behalf" (Micah 5:2).
"Jesus was born in Bethlehem in Judea..." (Matthew 2:1a).

"The Star" movie tells the story of Christmas from the donkey's perspective. It highlights some difficulties Joseph and Mary must have had traveling to Bethlehem on a donkey! I'm sure they asked themselves, "Lord, did you forget us? If we're following You, isn't it supposed to be easy?" As a mom, I can't help but think of all the preparation that goes into having a baby. A pregnant mom plans where her child will be born, decorates the nursery, chooses her doctor, thinks about names, and prays over the little baby in her womb. God did the same thing with Jesus. He planned all the details of His birth and life *long* before Mary even existed. God even planned where Jesus would be born.

As Mary and Joseph neared Joseph's hometown, the little town of Bethlehem, he likely passed familiar places that flooded him with memories. While in Bethlehem, Mary gave birth to Jesus, in a stable, of all places, just as God ordained. Long before, Micah had said "a ruler of Israel" would come from Bethlehem, "whose origins are in the distant past" (5:2). Jesus fulfilled that verse by being born in Bethlehem, the city of David. Bethlehem had origins in the past, since Israel's famed King David was also from Bethlehem. The word, Bethlehem means "house of bread," just as Jesus said He was the "Bread of Life" (John 6:35).

God used an ordinary couple and the unlikely place of a stable in a tiny town to birth the King of all Kings. Why? Places and people matter to God. God uses the small. It's one of His favorite things! He loves to use those who make Him big! If you find yourself feeling small this Christmas—because of a family member's words, circumstances, or something else—remember God's heart for the small. David was the youngest and littlest of his brothers. Bethlehem was an unheard-of town. God delights in using the small. Pray He will use you to make Him big this season. Christmas also often involves traveling to familiar places with memories. Be it a hometown, a familiar vacation spot, or a favorite corner of your house, allow God into those memories and places this season.

5

The Messiah Will Be Heir to David's Throne

"For the time is coming," says the LORD, when I will raise up a righteous descendant from King David's line. He will be a King who rules with wisdom. He will do what is just and right throughout the land" (Jeremiah 23:5)
"Jesus was known as the son of Joseph...the son of David...the son of God" (Luke 3:23-38).

Multiple studies have shown how knowing one's family history can aid in a child's success.[1] The book of Matthew starts out with a list of Jesus' family history. Ultimately, it shows that Jesus is a descendant of King David, who descended from Abraham. Everyone knew Jesus' family history. The Jews viewed which Israelite son's line they descended as a very important part of their identity. Since the prophet Jeremiah, the Jews had been looking forward to a

---

[1] https://selecthealth.org/blog/2019/08/5-benefits-of-knowing-your-family-history

Messiah, coming from King David's line, who would "rule with wisdom," as opposed to the harsh Assyrians, Babylonians, Meads, Persians, or Romans (Jeremiah 23:5). Jeremiah encouraged the people that God would send a Messiah who would "do what is just and right throughout the land," a promise they clung to in hard times (Jeremiah 23:5). Knowing Jesus will return again to rule the world is a promise we can hold fast to as well. Jesus, the ultimate King of Kings, will reign forever one day.

Jesus came from a long line of faith-filled family members. David was "a man after God's own heart," (Acts 13:22). Abraham, Isaac, and Jacob are all listed in the hall of faith in Hebrews 11. Not only that, but how many *kings* are mentioned in Jesus' genealogy in Mathew 1? A *lot!* Jesus' genealogy also had scandal.

- David with Bathsheba (Matthew 1:6)
- Boaz the daughter of Rahab prostitute
- Ruth the Moabite (Matthew 1:5)
- Judah and Tamar (Genesis 39, Matthew 1:3)

Yet through that very diverse and faith-filled royal family line, God birthed the King of Kings, Jesus.

King Charles of Britan comes from a long line of famous royals: Henry the 8th, Bloody Mary, Queen Elizabeth I and II, King George, Edward, and Queen Victoria, just to name a few. If you have accepted Christ into your heart, you have been adopted into His royal family (Romans 8, 11). You too, can have faith like Ruth, Rahab, and Abraham. This Christmas, consider those who do not have families to go home to. Consider inviting them into yours. Share about your royal lineage through Christ and invite them into that same royal line.

6
The Messiah Will Fulfill What the Passover Foreshadowed

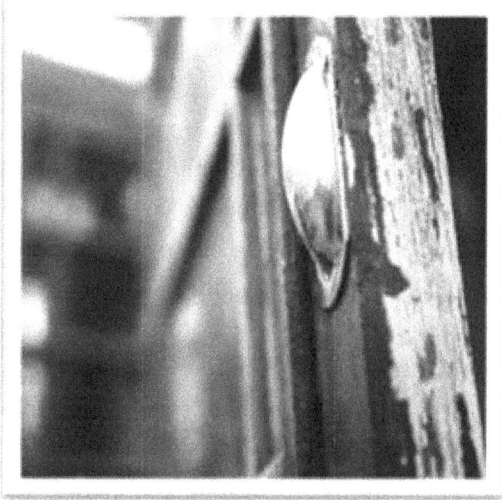

PC:
William
Krause

"On that night I will pass through the land of Egypt and strike down every firstborn son and firstborn male animal in the land of Egypt. I will execute judgment against all the gods of Egypt, for I am the LORD! But the blood on your doorposts will serve as a sign, marking the houses where you are staying. When I see the blood, I will pass over you. This plague of death will not touch you when I strike the land of Egypt" (Exodus 12:12-13).
"But God showed his great love for us by sending Christ to die for us while we were still sinners" (Romans 5:8).

After nine plagues on the Egyptian people, Pharaoh still refused to let the Israelite slaves go free. Then God sent an angel of death to kill every firstborn among all the families, *except* those who sacrificed a lamb and put the blood of the lamb over their doorway. God had told the Israelites if they did that, then He would *pass over* their homes. Preserving their lives required obedience to God. They had to *kill* a baby lamb with their own hands and a knife. Then they had to *eat* it! And smear its blood on the doorway to their house. Weird!

It's quite likely one wife said, "I just painted the door hot pink. Bloody red will clash. We're having company over tomorrow, and they don't know God, and we don't want to scare them off. Besides, my husband is working late tonight at the brick factory and I'm allergic to lambs, so we're just having bread instead." They lost their firstborn son for their disobedience. Did they not see the previous nine plagues? Did they not think God was serious? After they lost their firstborn son, did they finally believe? Or did they just think it was a coincidence? Some Israelites might not have believed God. But God stuck to His Word.

God fulfills His Word despite our belief. Many years later, the Israelites still celebrated the Passover. During one exceptional Passover celebration, Jesus, the ultimate Lamb of God, shed His blood on the cross so that God could pass over our sins (Exodus 12:13, Romans 5:8). He died so we can have life, just like the lambs died so that the firstborns could live.

The Israelites back then had a choice to make. We do too, even though we may not see such severe consequences so quickly for our disobedience. It's easy to make excuses during the holidays for why we do not spend time with God. It's the seemingly little, daily decisions that lead to either life or death. Not following the Lord will result in death. What choice have you made regarding that decision? Do you know someone who is headed for death? Have they made excuses for not following God, not knowing the consequences? Pray for them today.

7

The Messiah's Bones Will Not Be Broken

PC:
Daniel
Sandvik

"They must not leave any of the lamb until the next morning, and they must not break any of its bones. They must follow all the normal regulations concerning the Passover" (Numbers 9:12).

"So the soldiers came and broke the legs of the two men crucified with Jesus. But when they came to Jesus, they saw that he was already dead, so they didn't break his legs. One of the soldiers, however, pierced his side with a spear, and immediately blood and water flowed out. This report is from an eyewitness giving an accurate account. He speaks the truth so that you also may continue to believe.) These things happened in fulfillment of the Scriptures that say, 'Not one of his bones will be broken'" (John 19:32-36).

My children's school uniforms were so strict that I found it overwhelming. But the strictness had a unifying purpose across a racially and economically diverse student body.

Likewise, the Old Testament requirements for sacrifices might seem odd until we see the purpose.

A year after their exile from slavery, God had the Israelites celebrate through a ritual of remembrance (Numbers 9:1-3). Through sacrificing a lamb, again, without breaking its bones, they would remember doing that exact same thing one year prior. They would recall the thoughts in their head the year before. As the smell of roasted lamb hit their nose, they would recall the excitement they had a year prior when their two-year-old, who had just started to talk, said, "lamb"! At the sight of everyone eating the same meal they had eaten the previous year, they might recall trying to answer their children's questions: Why are we eating standing up? Why did we put blood on the doorway? Why didn't Judas' family put blood on the doorway? Is Judas going to die?

Along with the memories, a thankfulness would overwhelm them as they remembered being set free from slavery. Year after year, they would do this same ritual of remembrance to fix their eyes on the Lord and what He had done for them. The bones of the lamb would not be broken, because God had said so.

When the Jews saw Jesus, the Lamb of God, be sacrificed, they would remember the Passover lamb. When they saw that His bones were not broken, they would remember how the lamb's bones were not broken. They would know it was more than a fluke in the Roman execution. It was God's perfect will and design. It was because He truly was the Son of God!

What traditions do you have that remind you of what God has done for you? Do Christmas lights remind you how Jesus is the Light of the World? Does gift giving remind you of Jesus being the greatest gift of all? This Christmas, let your traditions point you to God. As you remember doing those traditions the previous year, praise God for all He's done this past year in your life.

The Messiah Will Be With Us

*"Call your councils of war, but they will be worthless.
Develop your strategies, but they will not succeed.
For God is with us" (Isaiah 8:10).*
*"All of this occurred to fulfill the Lord's message through
his prophet: 'Look! The virgin will conceive a child! She will
give birth to a son, and they will call him Immanuel, which
means 'God is with us''" (Matthew 1:22-23).*

The gods of other religions refer to themselves as being above humans, great and divine and different than humans, better than people. The God of Christianity is uniquely different in that a relationship with Him does not have to be earned and that He actually loves His people. He loves His people *so* much that He desires to be *with* us. Yes, He's different than us. He's perfect, omnipresent, omniscient, and all powerful. But He also loves us *so* much that He has gone to *great* lengths in order to be *with* us.

God sent His Son, as a baby, born of a virgin, in order that He could live with us. Instead of looking at people and being annoyed that they could not live up to His expectations, He reached down to help them succeed. He sent His Son to show us how to live. He sent Himself, in human form, as a baby. Instead of wiping us out and starting over, He chose to be with us on this crazy earth.

In the Old Testament, God had His people build a temple in order that He, a perfect being, could dwell with sinful man. He wanted to be with His people. He loved them so much. He really is a loving Father. Then, He sent Jesus, God Himself in human form, to live and walk among the people. After Jesus ascended into Heaven, God sent the Holy Spirit, who now resides in the hearts of men and women who follow Him. Our bodies are now temples of God. Because of Jesus' death and resurrection, we can now live with Christ in us, *with* us.

Immanuel means "God with us." It's one of Jesus's names. Sometimes it's spelled "Emmanuel." We hear it at Christmas-time. Christmas celebrates Jesus coming to earth as a baby, of God becoming a man, of God reaching down to us! No other god reaches down to his people. Every other god requires his people to reach up to him. Not the One True God, the Creator of the Universe. He created us because He loves us and wants to be with us. This Christmas, remember how the God of the Universe *loves* you and wants to be *with* you.

The Messiah Will Be Forsaken By God

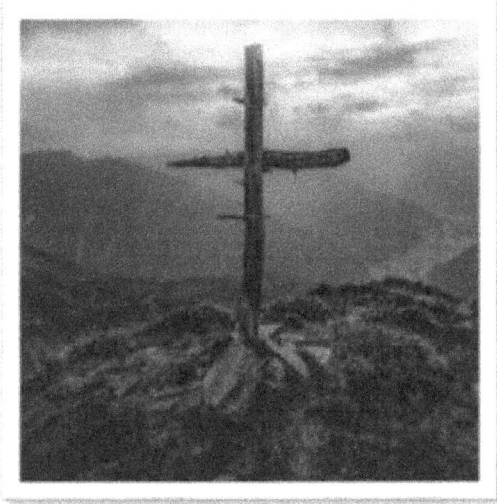

PC:
Eberhard

"My God, my God, why have you abandoned me? Why are you so far away when I groan for help" (Psalms 22:1)
"At about three o'clock, Jesus called out with a loud voice, 'Eli, Eli, lema sabachthani?" which means "My God, my God, why have you abandoned me?"" (Matthew 27:46).

Unspeakable pain. Have you ever been in so much pain you could not even speak? What did you do? One time, I endured so much pain that all I could do was say, "PRAY!" to the person next to me. Jesus knows such pain.

When Jesus walked the earth, young Jewish boys memorized the Torah and the Psalms. However, they didn't label the Psalms with numbers like we do today. Instead, the first line of each Psalm was the name of the Psalm. When Jesus said from the cross, "My God, my God, why have you abandoned me," He was not simply crying out to God. He was referencing the entirety of Psalm 22 (Matthew 27:46).

He likely did feel abandoned by God. Yet He was God all at the same time. Can you imagine the self-control to have the ability to stop your own deathly pain, and yet choose not to? Wow. Jesus was in so much pain on the cross, He couldn't speak. How do I know? Because if He could, He would have been preaching a sermon from up there! Instead of preaching a sermon, He simply got the words out that referenced the one Psalm that said all the things He desired to say, but was unable to, because of His chosen willful suffering humanity. He said the first line to Psalm 22.

If you read over Psalm 22, it says, "they pierced my hands and my feet" (Psalm 22:16). Jesus's enemies cast lots for His clothing (Psalm 22:18). It wasn't just an emotional Psalm. It really happened to Jesus. They pierced His hands and feet. They cast lots for His clothing. God knew it would happen and gave us that Psalm and many other prophecies to remind His people of His Sovereignty in the midst of the chaos of losing their beloved spiritual leader.

In the midst of the chaos of the holiday season, what promises of God do you need to remember? That you are loved (John 3:16)? That He is in control (Colossians 1:16-17)? That Jesus will return to make all things right (Revelation 21:5)? Whatever chaos you endure, even if it's just an unsettled spirit, I pray you allow God's truth and peace to comfort you today.

10
The Messiah Will Be a Descendant of Abraham, Isaah, and Jacob

"And through your [Abraham's] descendants all the nations of the earth will be blessed—all because you have obeyed me" (Genesis 22:18).

"God gave the promises to Abraham and his child. And notice that the Scripture doesn't say 'to his children,' as if it meant many descendants. Rather, it says 'to his child'—and that, of course, means Christ" (Galatians 3:16).

Someone told D.L. Moody, "The world has yet to see what God will do with one man who is fully devoted to Him." Moody then set out to see what God would do with him if he fully devoted himself to the Lord. Over time, he started inner city ministries, Sunday schools, Moody Church and the Moody Bible Institute—from which many ministries spread all over the world.

Never underestimate the power of one person walking with the Lord on a daily basis. Never underestimate what God can do with you when you make Him the center of your life. God blessed all the nations of the world through Jesus, Abraham's seed (Genesis 22:18)! Because of Jesus, *everyone* has access to God. It's not about how much money you make, what family you came from, your race, or even your religion. We all have the opportunity to have a relationship with God. Abraham made some big mistakes. But Abraham chose to trust God. Therefore, God used Abraham and blessed him greatly! If God did that with Abraham, just imagine what He can do with you.

You too can be used of God, today. D.L. Moody shared his faith every day with someone who did not know Christ. Like brushing his teeth daily or doing the dishes, He had a daily habit of sharing Christ with those who did not know Him. How often does your heart ache for people in your life who do not know Christ? How often do you pray for them to know Christ? Pray God could use you to bring them into a saving knowledge of Christ. We can offer our imperfect selves to God for daily obedience to Him. As we rely on His perfect strength, we can steps one day at a time to see what He will do as we fully commit our days to Him. As you go through the holiday season, beyond just remembering the traditions and making Christ the center of your celebrations, remember the importance your own walk with the Lord. Also remember to invite others into that, so they can experience Christ for themselves. That's the ultimate way we bless others and are ourselves blessed.

The Messiah will be the Lion from Judah

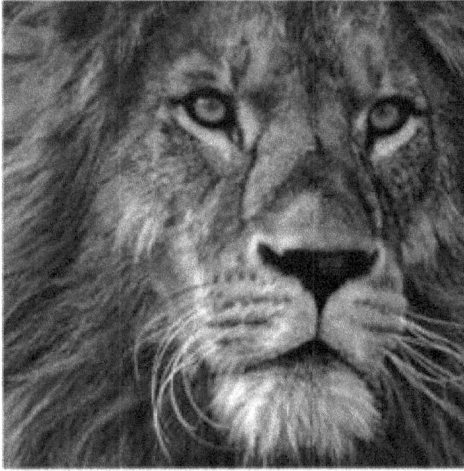

"Judah, my son, is a young lion that has finished eating its prey. Like a lion he crouches and lies down; like a lioness— who dares to rouse him?" (Genesis 49:9).

"But one of the twenty-four elders said to me, 'Stop weeping! Look, the Lion of the tribe of Judah, the heir to David's throne, has won the victory. He is worthy to open the scroll and its seven seals'" (Revelation 5:5).

Have you ever seen a lamb placed inside the lion's area at the zoo? Me neither. Why not? I know you know, but let's say it together. Because the lion would *devour* the helpless little lamb! Sheep are not the smartest or bravest animals. Yet Jesus is described as both a lion and a lamb (Revelation 5:5-6). He's fierce and also gentle. He allowed Himself to be slain, like a lamb. Yet He defeated death like a lion.

In Genesis, Jacob gathered his twelve sons and two grandsons to his bedside before he died. He passed on blessings to each of them, well, mostly blessings! Jacob described Judah, the fourth born, as a lion, in whom the scepter would not depart until it came to...Jesus (Genesis 49:10). In other words, he viewed Judah as mighty. From Judah's family line, Jesus would be born, to save the world. Jesus descended from the tribe of Judah.

Revelation gives us a glimpse into what will happen in Heaven and on earth in the last days. One of those things happening in Heaven involves God on His throne having a scroll that needs to be opened. But only someone worthy can open it. For a moment, no one appears to be found to be worthy! Then, with great suspense, it is revealed that the lion of the tribe of Judah is worthy, because He conquered the grave (Revelation 5:5). He appears, looking like a lamb who has been slain, ready to open the scroll (Revelation 5:6).

Jesus was to come from the tribe of Judah, and He did. Even at the end of time, they referred to Him as the lion of Judah. Both a lion and a lamb, He came to us as a baby and left conquering death! Do you prefer to view Jesus as a lion or a lamb? Can you picture Him as both? Willing to be vulnerable like a baby and submissive to death on a cross, yet powerful enough to defeat sin in your own life? Do you have little lambs or kids in your life? Can you help them grow up to be lions defeating sin and death? This Christmas, remember Jesus as both the lion and the lamb.

12
The Messiah Will Spend a Season in Egypt

"When Israel was a child, I loved him, and I called my son out of Egypt" (Hosea 11:1).

"After the wise men were gone, an angel of the Lord appeared to Joseph in a dream. 'Get up! Flee to Egypt with the child and his mother,' the angel said. 'Stay there until I tell you to return, because Herod is going to search for the child to kill him.' That night Joseph left for Egypt with the child and Mary, his mother, and they stayed there until Herod's death. This fulfilled what the Lord had spoken through the prophet: 'I called my Son out of Egypt'"
(Matthew 2:13-15).

Pregnant women have regular appointments to check on the well-being of their babies. The checkups continue throughout the babies' first few years of life due to their extreme vulnerability. God sent His own Son to earth as a baby, the most vulnerable of human beings.

Our Old Testament verse from Hosea mentions God calling His Son, Israel, out of Egypt (11:1). We normally just think of God's Son as Jesus, but the Lord also referred to Israel as His firstborn Son. *How can God have two firstborn Sons?* He's God. That's how. The Hosea verse has two fulfillments. God called His child, Israel, out of slavery in Egypt, through the parting of the Red Sea (Exodus 14). However, according to Matthew 2:13-15, the Hosea verse also refers to *Jesus!* When Jesus was a baby, King Herod went on a killing spree, murdering every boy two years old and younger in and around Bethlehem. Thankfully, the Lord sent an angel to Joseph who directed him to Egypt where Jesus was kept safe. Then the Lord called Jesus out of Egypt, just as He had called His son, Israel, years earlier out of slavery in Egypt.

Christmas celebrates Jesus's birth. God sent His Son as a vulnerable baby into the hands of a young couple who had never been parents before, and had likely been abandoned by their extended family. Following God does not mean life will be easy, unfortunately. Protecting baby Jesus without familial help would have been difficult. Yet Mary and Joseph were never alone. God promises to be with us always (Matthew 28:20). To avoid King Herod's killing spree, God miraculously intervened by directing Joseph to take his family to Egypt. Going to Egypt with a wee one could not have been easy, especially on such short notice! Joseph and Mary had not sinned. God had a greater purpose in mind than making their life easy. The hard in their world had nothing to do with them—except that they had been chosen for something good! The hard in their life resulted from a sinful jealous ruler acting poorly.

As you celebrate the birth of Christ, remember how God miraculously rescued Jesus as a baby so that He could save you from your sins.

13
A Messenger Will Prepare the Way for the Messiah

*"Listen! It's the voice of someone shouting, "Clear the way
through the wilderness for the Lord! Make a straight
highway through the wasteland for our God" (Isaiah 40:3).
"John replied in the words of the prophet Isaiah: 'I am a
voice shouting in the wilderness, 'Clear the way for
the Lord's coming!'"" (John 1:23).*

My dad owned a seal coating, paving, and striping
business for over thirty years. He used to say, "we cover all
your pavement maintenance needs." If you had a grass
driveway and wanted a paved one, he could fix that. If you
had pot holes and needed them filled, he could fix that. He
painted lines on parking lots, roads, and highways as well.
What he did made driving easier for people. It made parking
easier. His work made the roads level so people in their cars
had a smooth ride.

At the time of Jesus, the king hired people like my dad whenever he wanted to go somewhere. Those hired would be in charge of making sure the roads where the king traveled were smooth. This gave the king a nice gentle ride, one without bumps.

John instructed the people to do that for the Lord, the most-high King. They were to clear a path for the Lord to travel through. They were to "make a straight highway" (Isaiah 40:3). John's ministry cleared the way for Jesus and prepared the peoples' hearts. Jesus's success had a lot to do with John getting the people ready.

John encouraged people in the wilderness, the wasteland. He preached where the Word was not known. He blazed the trail for which Jesus walked through. John readied the people to receive Jesus. Some of us are called to be trailblazers, like John. Others are called to be harvesters, to reap what others have sown, like Jesus. Which do you feel God calling you to?

Today, I feel God calling me to grow my tiny part-time gig into something that can provide a full salary. I feel led to be a trailblazer. Even though some days I think following someone else's path would be easier, I have to follow God's call for me.

What is God calling you to this Christmas? How can you smooth the way for yourself or someone else to come to Jesus? Or how can you harvest what others have sown? Is God calling you to invite someone over for the holidays? Or is there a conversation that needs to happen? Does someone need to be asked if they truly know Jesus and are ready to meet Him?

14
The Messiah Will Be Rejected by His Own People

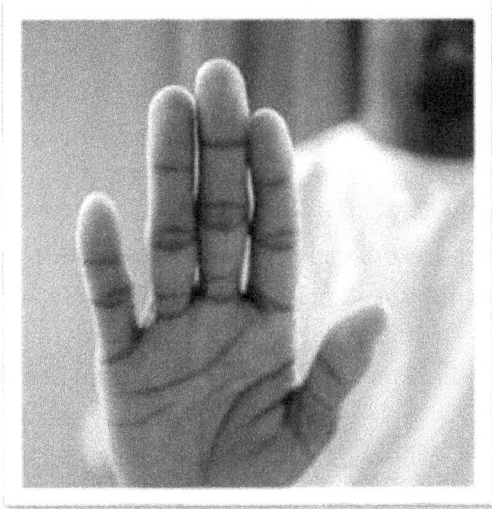

PC:
Monstera
Production

"Even my own brothers pretend they don't know me; they treat me like a stranger" (Psalms 69:8).
"For even his brothers didn't believe in him." (John 7:5).

The phrase, "I don't know you right now," has become the phrase we use when someone does something of which we disapprove. The Jew-and even Jesus' actual family-disowned Him because they did not approve of Him. They did not understand. They did not get it. He was not normal! Why would he leave the comfy carpenter shop his father had set up for him? He was the best carpenter Nazareth had ever seen! His business could have been booming! Did Jesus care nothing for His family? Jesus, the eldest son, was to care for His momma after Joseph died! How could He leave for some unheard-of preaching journey? Some thought that, anyway.

We might not know the exact choice words exchanged, but we do know His family did not approve of His career choice. In fact, they pretended not to know Him (Psalm 69:8). Not only as their brother, but as the Messiah (John 1:11, 7:5). Can you imagine? Their brother was famous, with 5,000 followers, the maximum amount allowed for a personal Facebook account. Famous He was, but eating, He was not (Mark 3:20). The Bible says that at times, Jesus was too busy to eat. What Jewish boy did not eat? It was tradition to eat! Did He not watch *Fiddler on the Roof* and see all that feasting and togetherness with family? His momma raised Him better than that! We do not always understand God's ways.

Do you have people in your life by whom you feel misunderstood? Have they disowned you or do you fear they will if you follow God's leading? Will you see some of them this Christmas season, at a spouse's holiday party, a family gathering, or a neighborhood Christmas party? Be encouraged that Jesus gets it. He gets you. He understands. He sees. He approves of you and has the best life ready for you. He is enough. You are too. You can trust Him. You can step out in faith today because He is with you (Matthew 28:18-20). He will never leave you nor forsake you (Hebrews 13:5). Because Jesus sees us, we can give others the gift of being seen and understood this Christmas too.

15
The Messiah Will Be a Prophet

"I will raise up a prophet like you from among their fellow Israelites. I will put my words in his mouth, and he will tell the people everything I command him" (Deuteronomy 18:18).

"Then times of refreshment will come from the presence of the Lord, and he will again send you Jesus, your appointed Messiah. For he must remain in heaven until the time for the final restoration of all things, as God promised long ago through his holy prophets. Moses said, 'The Lord your God will raise up for you a Prophet like me from among your own people. Listen carefully to everything he tells you. Then Moses said, 'Anyone who will not listen to that Prophet will be completely cut off from God's people'" (Acts 3:20-23).

It's so easy to read the Old Testament prophecies about Jesus and think, "Yeah, I guess that could be talking about a

Messiah." However, the *New* Testament writers explained the Old Testament prophecies so that we can confidently say, "Whoa! That's about Jesus!" The New Testament writers decoded the Old Testament mysteries.

Our Old Testament passage from Jeremiah today says God will raise up a prophet. While it sounds like Jesus, it would be easy to contend, "Nah, it was Jeremiah. Maybe Micah. Nahum was the prophet being talked about there." When in doubt, look to the Bible. Often, the Bible answers the very questions we have *about* the Bible. In Acts 3:20-23, it says, "Moses said, 'The Lord your God will raise up for you a Prophet like me from among your own people. Listen carefully to everything he tells you.'" Luke, the writer of Acts, reminded the people how the Old Testament prophecy written by Moses in Deuteronomy had been fulfilled in the life of Jesus.

"A prophet like Moses" meant a deliverer (Acts 3:22). Moses delivered the Israelites from actual slavery just like Jesus delivered us from our slavery to sin! Jesus, a prophet *like* Moses, was the sacrificial lamb that saved everyone's lives. Moses was an Israelite raised up to rescue the Israelites. Jesus was an Israelite too, raised up to save all people. Jesus was raised up among His fellow Israelites, *just* like the verse prophesied!

Was Jesus a prophet? Jesus *did* prophesy about the future! He spoke about His crucifixion and resurrection before they happened. Those prophesies have already been fulfilled. Jesus also spoke about His second coming and the end times. His Word can be trusted. What He said will happen. Since as a prophet, He knows the future, we can trust Him with our future.

"Prophet" only speaks to one of Jesus's attributes. Listening to all He said means submitting to His Lordship as

God. Do you simply view Jesus as a prophet? Or as the LORD of your life? How about those around you? What would change this season if you or those around you viewed Jesus as LORD and trusted Him with your future since He, as the ultimate prophet, knows the future?

The Messiah Will Be Preceded By Elijah

PC:
Kelly
Sikkema

"Look, I am sending you the prophet Elijah before the great and dreadful day of the Lord arrives. His preaching will turn the hearts of fathers to their children, and the hearts of children to their fathers. Otherwise I will come and strike the land with a curse" (Malachi 4:5-6).
"For before John came, all the prophets and the law of Moses looked forward to this present time. And if you are willing to accept what I say, he is Elijah, the one the prophets said would come" (Matthew 11:13-14).

Before going to camp for the whole summer at age twelve, my mom told me, "Be sure not to chew too much gum! I hear it will hurt your jaw!" Another year, her last words were, "Don't wear those hair ties on your wrist! I read that it could cause cancer." At nineteen, before getting on a plane to spend a summer in China, I remember her pleading, "Please. [Dramatic pause] DON'T EAT DOG!" Twenty years later, I still remember her famous last words. I thought about her last words for months before I saw her again.

Today's Malachi verses contain the last words of the Old Testament. They were His final words before Jesus came to earth. Malachi told the people that God would send the prophet Elijah back to turn the hearts of the fathers to their children and the children to their fathers (Malachi 4:5-6). Family unity would be restored. That would happen *before* the Old Testament prophecies about the "great and dreadful day of the Lord," (Malachi 4:5). It gave the people hope! God had *good* in store for them. God had given His people something to look forward to!

The people had four hundred years to think about those verses before He spoke again! The Lord knew the people would stray, but some would remain faithful. He gave the last words in Malachi for the remnant, to remind them that He had not forgotten them. In the book of Matthew, we see the fulfillment of the Malachi verse through John the Baptist, "the Elijah who was to come" (11:11-15). The people remembered. They remembered God's final message to them and found hope in Jesus explaining its fulfillment. Some did not believe it, but many did! Jesus would return to make all things right.

How much do we look forward to Christmas? Our Christmas decorations go up at least by the day after Thanksgiving, if not earlier! We look forward to Christmas vacations, presents, togetherness, refreshment, good food, parties, snow covered pine trees, and joy-filled seasons. What about Christmas do you look forward to the most? How much more can we look forward to Christ's second return, when He will make all things right for a final time.

17
The Messiah Will Speak in Parables

"For I will speak to you in a parable. I will teach you hidden lessons from our past" (Psalms 78:2).
"Jesus always used stories and illustrations like these when speaking to the crowds. In fact, he never spoke to them without using such parables. This fulfilled what God had spoken through the prophet: 'I will speak to you in parables. I will explain things hidden since the creation of the world'" (Matthew 13:34-35).

I wonder if Jesus woke up each day thinking, "which Old Testament prophecies will I fulfill today?" Or if He pondered how to disciple the disciples like a parent ponders how to get their child to understand a concept.

The Old Testament predicted that Jesus would speak in parables! A parable is "a story or saying that illustrates a truth using comparison, hyperbole, or simile...[and] can be a model, analogy, or example..." according to the Lexham

Bible Dictionary. You might think of the parable of the lost sheep or the prodigal son in Luke 15. Some places in the Bible where the word, "parable" appears, it could have come from the root word meaning "riddle."

A riddle is defined as "an interrogative statement that seeks to obscure its referent with the goal that the audience will name the referent" according to the Lexham Bible Dictionary. Does the definition of a riddle sound like a riddle to you? With a referent here and a referent there, I think we need a referee to keep everyone in line! Obscure means to hide and a referent is like making a reference.[2] Reread the verses above with that in mind.

As Jesus spoke to the people in parables, He *revealed* the Bible and *Himself* to them. He did not do that to confuse people, but to reference things the Bible already said. Those who knew God's Word would understand and make the connections. The hidden things would be revealed to them. But those who did not really believe the Bible would not have understood Jesus' references. The hidden things were revealed through Jesus's use of parables to those He desired to grant understanding.

Are there parts to the Christmas story you do not understand? Can you believe that most of history the Bible stories have been passed down orally without a written Word? Praise God for giving us His Word with an abundance of resources to help us understand it! Pray for those who do not yet have access to God's Word in their own language, or those who cannot read. Consider how you can disciple someone today by explaining the Christmas story to them. Consider explaining it to a child, too young to read.

---

[2] https://www.merriam-webster.com/dictionary/obscure
https://www.merriam-webster.com/dictionary/referent

18
The Messiah Will Heal the Brokenhearted

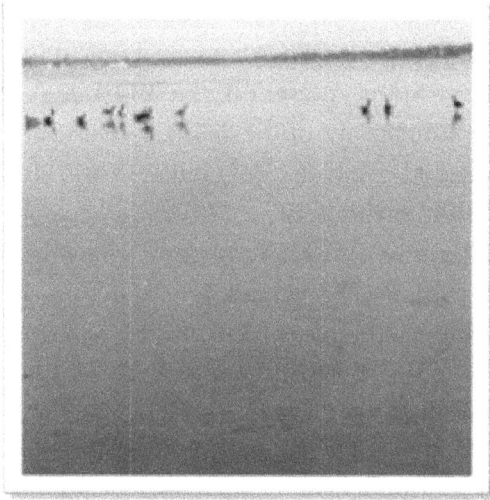

"The Spirit of the Sovereign Lord is upon me, for the Lord has anointed me to bring good news to the poor. He has sent me to comfort the brokenhearted and to proclaim that captives will be released and prisoners will be freed" (Isaiah 61:1).

"The Spirit of the Lord is upon me, for he has anointed me to bring Good News to the poor. He has sent me to proclaim that captives will be released, that the blind will see, that the oppressed will be set free, and that the time of the Lord's favor has come" (Luke 4:18-19).

Ahhh! I LOVE this Isaiah verse! I love it because of *how* Jesus *fulfilled* it! Read Luke 4. The Bible's Words are better than mine. Let's recap. Jesus was led away in the desert to be tempted for forty days. Note: God led Jesus somewhere, in the desert, where He was tempted to sin. If you feel like you are in the desert and tempted to sin, do not automatically feel that it is a result of you doing something wrong! God very well could have led *you* there just as He led our Lord Jesus there. After forty days, Word spread quickly, and everyone was attracted to Jesus's teaching because Jesus returned "filled with the Holy Spirit's power" (Luke 4:14-15). Note that you too can be brought out of the desert by God, filled with the Holy Spirit and ready to do God's Work. Just pass the temptation test. Stand firm!

Then Jesus went to His hometown where they had heard about Him on Facebook and followed His social media pages. While there, Jesus went to the Synagogue on the Sabbath to teach. Everyone showed up to listen. He was handed a scroll of the Bible to read. He read the above verse from Isaiah. Then He sat down and said, "The Scripture you've just heard has been fulfilled this very day" (Luke 4:21)!

At first the crowd was excited. But as Jesus explained more, they became furious! They even formed a mob and tried to throw Jesus off a cliff! For real! That's what Jesus got for preaching good news! Jesus preached that being poor was not a result of someone's sin! Jesus preached comfort for the brokenhearted, that everyone had access to Heaven, and people no longer had to struggle alone. Hard times were not the direct result of sin. Captives to sin could be released. Prisoners of Satan could be set free!

But many who heard the good news rejected it.

What will you do with the good news of Jesus this Christmas? Take comfort for your own broken heart? Reach out to your church for help being freed from sin? Share this message with the poor? Whatever you do, don't throw it off a cliff. Accept it. Share it. Believe it.

19

The Messiah will Restore the Gentiles to Himself

PC:
Richard
Seibert

"He says, 'You will do more than restore the people of Israel to me. I will make you a light to the Gentiles, and you will bring my salvation to the ends of the earth'" (Isaiah 49:6).
"He is a light to reveal God to the nations, and he is the glory of your people Israel!" (Luke 2:32).

Kroger advertised "Fresh for Everyone" during a time of intense division in America. They said things like, "Fresh is for people who eat. Yes, that's you." Cartoon people of every racial and ethnic background were pictured on banners in grocery stores everywhere. A commercial showed a biracial couple hosting many foreign exchange students cooking ethnic meals as a way to connect with their students.

It's rare that a message is so cross-culturally accepted in America. Imagine Jesus's challenge to save the world--with all is diversity! He came as a Jew. The people in Jesus's day were divided into two camps: Jews or Gentiles. The Lord declared that Jesus would "do more than restore the [Jews] to [God]" (Isaiah 49:6). He would also be "a light to the Gentiles" and bring salvation to *everyone!* Fresh salvation for all who eat. Yes, that's you!

Mary and Joseph likely felt like outcasts when people disapproved of their out-of-wedlock pregnancy. The angel did not appear to everyone, only them and the shepherds. After surviving their first week as parents with a newborn, they somehow made it to Jerusalem, keeping their faith in order to have their baby boy circumcised on the eighth day (Genesis 17:12). While today circumcision happens at a hospital, then it happened by a rabbi at the temple.

During their visit to the temple, Simeon saw the young family and "took" Jesus in his arms and started praising God (Luke 2:28). He quoted Isaiah, again reiterating that Jesus would bring salvation to *everyone.* Simeon's words said that Jesus would be a light to the nations, that He would reach the world, with all its diversity. Mary and Joesph, who likely felt left out and like outcasts, had birthed a boy who would reach the outcast. He would reach the Gentiles as the Jews were always meant to. Jesus would reach *everyone.*

Do you believe you are included in everyone? Is there someone you know who you feel has been excluded and needs to be reminded that Jesus came for them too? How can you remind them today? God still sees His people in only two categories: those who know Him and those who do not.

20

The Messiah Will Be a Priest in the Order of Melchizedek

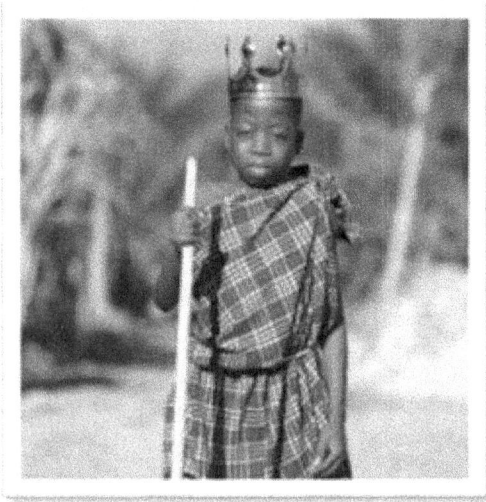

PC:
Safari
Consoler

"The Lord has taken an oath and will not break his vow:
'You are a priest forever in the order of Melchizedek'"
(Psalms 110:4).
"That is why Christ did not honor himself by assuming he
could become High Priest. No, he was chosen by God, who
said to him, 'You are my Son. Today I have become your
Father.' And in another passage God said to him, 'You are a
priest forever in the order of Melchizedek'"
(Hebrews 5:5-6).

Many things, even after explained, still leave us with so
many questions, like Melchizedek, the mysterious priest in
the Bible around the time of Abraham. Where did
Melchizedek come from? If the temple were not a thing yet,
who made Him priest? And of what? We first see Abraham
with Melchizedek after winning a fierce battle. "And
Melchizedek, the king of Salem and a priest of God Most

High, brought Abram some bread and wine. Melchizedek blessed Abram with this blessing: 'Blessed be Abram by God Most High, Creator of heaven and earth. And blessed be God Most High, who has defeated your enemies for you.'" Then Abram gave Melchizedek a tenth of all the goods he had recovered" (Genesis 14:18-20).

God appointed Melchizedek as priest, but was he the first? I think one of

Abraham's descendants forgot to include that detail in passing down the family history. Maybe it was such common knowledge at the time that they did not think of passing down such obvious information. Melchizedek is the first priest we read about in the Bible. Jesus also was a priest appointed by God (Hebrews 5:5-6). Priests offered sacrifices for the people. Jesus was a sacrifice. Jesus too, like Melchizedek, offered bread and wine to his disciples the night before he died.

Jesus and Melchizedek were both appointed to their priestly positions by God. Believers today are also appointed as priests (1 Peter 2:5). We do not offer bloody sacrifices today. No person has the ability to take people's sins away. But we have the message of Jesus that we can share with others on His behalf in order to bring people to Jesus, so that their sins can be forgiven. We have priestly duties (as Jack Black from *Nacho Liebre* says), to stand in the gap between God and people who don't know Him. Jesus is the forever priest between God and man. We are His forever priests that get to point people to Him.

In the hustle and bustle of the season, ask yourself what parts of the Bible you still do not understand and pray that God would grant you a deeper understanding of those things. Also think about how you can point someone to Jesus today like the priests used to point the people to God.

21
The Messiah Will Reach Outsiders

PC:
Jenny
Herman

"You have taught children and infants to tell of your strength, silencing your enemies and all who oppose you" (Psalms 8:2).
"The blind and the lame came to him in the Temple, and he healed them. The leading priests and the teachers of religious law saw these wonderful miracles and heard even the children in the Temple shouting, 'Praise God for the Son of David.'
But the leaders were indignant. They asked Jesus, 'Do you hear what these children are saying?'
'Yes,' Jesus replied. 'Haven't you ever read the Scriptures? For they say, 'You have taught children and infants to give you praise'"" (Matthew 21:14-16).

Picture it: Jesus went into the temple, meant for worshiping God, and cleared out the money changers, using a whip meant for livestock! They were basically having an animal auction. Then he started healing people, and a crowd formed. The children in the crowd started shouting "Praise God for the Son of David" (Matthew 21:15). Then, the religious leaders got all upset about it! They were "indignant" (Matthew 21:15). They were angry at the "injustice" of it all. Wait, what injustice? Their casino being shut down? Jesus receiving attention from little children? Them not being the center of attention? Them not having control over the situation? Having to make deals on trading livestock *outside*, in the sun as opposed to in the nicely furnished and polished temple? They asked Jesus if he knew what the children were saying. Bahaha. He knows everything! He's God! But to them He was just a man. Jesus responded with, "Yes," (Matthew 21:16). Then He asked the religious leaders pointedly, "Haven't you ever read the Scriptures? For they say, 'You have taught children and infants to give you praise'" quoting from Psalm 8:2 (Matthew 21:16).

Jesus responded to the religious leaders by quoting the Bible, something they should have known well. He spoke their language. Haven't you read? Don't you get it? I AM the Son of David. I AM the fulfillment of these prophecies. I AM your answer. No, Jesus didn't say it quite like that. He simply pointed them back to the Bible prophecies about Himself, hoping they would see. Then He left. It's a good example for us. We don't have to stay and argue or give a long explanation to everyone. We can be brief and then move on. If they want more information, or are sincerely interested, they will ask.

The holidays often bring up tension between family members. Just know that you do not have to engage an argument with an indignant person. You too, can answer simply and politely and then walk away. Jesus did, and you can too. Looking at these verses also shows us Jesus's love for children. He found value in what they were saying. He didn't want them silenced. How can you give a child room to be heard today?

22
The Messiah Will Be Falsely Accused

"Malicious witnesses testify against me. They accuse me of crimes I know nothing about" (Psalms 35:11).
"Finally, some men stood up and gave this false testimony: 'We heard him say, 'I will destroy this Temple made with human hands, and in three days I will build another, made without human hands''" (Mark 14:57-58).

While we celebrate Jesus' birth at Christmas, without His death and resurrection, His birth would mean next to nothing. Before being crucified by the Romans, Jesus had to face a Jewish trial. Instead of waiting until the morning, everyone needed for a court "had gathered," for a special middle of the night kangaroo court trial because Jesus's threat to their way of life needed to be dealt with *immediately* (Mark 14:53).

"Inside, the leading priests and the entire high council were trying to find evidence against Jesus, so they could put him to death. But they couldn't find any. Many false witnesses spoke against him, but they contradicted each other. Finally, some men stood up and gave this false testimony" (Mark 14:55-57).

Can you imagine the fierceness of the anti-Jesus mob? It was no peaceful protest. They had murder on their minds. They arrested Jesus as soon as Judas told them His location. They arranged all the key people in order to "legally" falsely accuse Him right away. Jesus had done nothing wrong, yet everyone was against Him. Those against Him had not listened to Jesus's message on loving your enemies. In one ear and out the other. But God was in control, even though Jesus had relinquished His eternal ability to stop the whole thing. Jesus used all of His godliness to refrain from using His godliness to limit His own unjust pain.

The Old Testament prophesied that Jesus would be falsely accused. The leading priests could not find any evidence against Jesus when they accused Him. Yet Jesus also did not stop the opposition, but simply endured it. At other times in the Bible, He responded, but sometimes He simply walked away. Either way, He never responded in the anger in which they came to Him. Remember, they found no evidence for which to accuse Jesus. He was and is perfect. Let it be that way with us. Let us live such pure and holy, bold and graceful lives that people have to lie about us in order to accuse us of anything. Pray for divine wisdom in knowing how to respond as you face different types of people and possible opposition this season.

23

The Messiah Will Have His Hands, Feet, and Side Pierced

PC:
Mario
Mendez

"My enemies surround me like a pack of dogs; an evil gang closes in on me. They have pierced my hands and feet" (Psalm 22:16).
"They told him, 'We have seen the Lord!' But he replied, 'I won't believe it unless I see the nail wounds in his hands, put my fingers into them, and place my hand into the wound in his side'" (John 20:25).

Have you ever fell in love with a song because you so resonated with its lyrics? Songs often speak the words our hearts feel. While we do not entirely know how Jesus felt on the cross, He did say the first line to a song, Psalm 22, while on the cross. That reference would have led good Jews to continue reciting the rest of that Psalm. It would be similar if someone said the line to a famous song and you finished singing it for them.

The Jews reciting the Psalm would have recited the Psalm about Jesus's hands and feet being pierced as they watched Jesus hanging from the cross with His hands and feet having been pierced. Would they have made the connection that Jesus is the Son of God? Or would they have just thought it was another neat coincidence? Thomas, a disciple in the New Testament, refused to believe Jesus had risen from the dead until he could touch Jesus' hands and feel the nail marks. He must have been out fetching lunch when Jesus appeared to the rest of the disciples. But Thomas did not care what they had to say about it. He wanted hard core evidence. Jesus did not condemn Thomas, but appeared to Thomas too, and told him to touch and believe.

Jesus's death was prophesied. His hands and feet were pierced, as prophesied. He died and rose again, as prophesied. As a result, we forever celebrate not only His resurrection, but His birth, with songs. Some Christmas songs are silly, but some are full of deep Biblical truth. "Oh Little Town of Bethlehem" reminds us how our Savior came from a *tiny* nobody town in a tiny country in the middle of an oppressive Roman regime. "Joy to the World," reminds us of the hope Jesus coming into the world brought. "Emmanuel" reminds us of how our God desires to be *with* us. What is your favorite Christmas carol and why? The next time you hear a Christmas song that reminds you of some truth about Christ, meditate on it. Let the truth sink deep into your conscience. Ask yourself if you believe it and pray that you could live like it.

24

The Messiah Will Be Called King

PC:

Alexey

Makh-

inko

"For the Lord declares, 'I have placed my chosen king on the throne in Jerusalem, on my holy mountain'" (Psalms 2:6).

"A sign was fastened above Jesus' head, announcing the charge against him. It read: 'This is Jesus, the King of the Jews'" (Matthew 27:37).

Billy and Tish named their baby girl, "Destiny Hope." Since she smiled all the time, they nicknamed her, "Smiley." The nickname became such a part of her identity that when she got older, she officially changed her name to "Miley." Today, we know her as Miley Cyrus. Miley's parents had no idea when they nicknamed their baby girl "Smiley," that someday the world would know her as "Miley." But they gave her a nickname, that fit her perfectly, and later she became known for it.

Likewise, the Roman soldiers gave Jesus the nickname "King" as they wrote it on a sign above Jesus' head, little knowing that one day He would be known as the ultimate King. Psalm 2:6 talks of Jesus being referred to as God's King, placed on God's "holy mountain." That's where Abraham nearly sacrificed his only son, Isaac. God foretold the exact location of where His Son would die, long before crucifixions were even a thing. Psalm 2 also explained God's attitude toward the nations as opposed to His preference for His own Son. God warned the nations and other kings of the world in Psalm 2, to pay attention to *His* Son, to *His* King.

Christmas focuses on baby Jesus. These passages remind us of His kingship. A historical king had people's heads chopped off just because he disliked them. People watched what they said and did in the presence of the king. They respected the king, out of reverence, fear, and a respect for the power of position. Our culture often has a "what can they do to me?" attitude when approaching authority. The nations in Psalm 2 had that type of attitude toward God. God rebuked the nations and pointed them toward His Son and King (Psalm 2).

What's your attitude toward Jesus as King? If someone pinned a nickname over your head this month, what would it be? Hurried? Overspent? Snappy, Restful, Joyful? What would you want it to be? Every time you feel there's not enough time, patience, grace, or Christmas spirit to go around, think on Jesus as King. He's still King of the world. Let Him be King of your world, of your day, of your moments.

25
The Messiah Will Ride on a Donkey

PC:

Pixaby

"Rejoice, O people of Zion! Shout in triumph, O people of Jerusalem! Look, your king is coming to you. He is righteous and victorious, yet he is humble, riding on a donkey—riding on a donkey's colt" (Zechariah 9:9).
"Then they brought the colt to Jesus and threw their garments over it, and he sat on it. Many in the crowd spread their garments on the road ahead of him, and others spread leafy branches they had cut in the fields. Jesus was in the center of the procession, and the people all around him were shouting, 'Praise God! Blessings on the one who comes in the name of the Lord! Blessings on the coming Kingdom of our ancestor David! Praise God in highest heaven!'" (Mark 11:7-10).

When my town has a parade, the streets are closed and everyone lines up to watch. The children hold bags ready to catch candy thrown to them from those in the parades.

Similarly, when Jesus paraded through town on a donkey, it seemed planned. Why? Was there a notice in the local paper about a one-man donkey parade? Did the disciples advertise it on Instagram? Was there a Costco free sample special if you showed up? Like, where did all the people come from? How did they know to call Jesus "Hosanna in the highest?" Where did He get *that* nickname? Are you ready for the answer?

It.

Was.

Prophesied!

It was prophesied. Even to the exact day Jesus would come through, was prophesied. They were waiting for the Messiah to come that day, riding on a donkey. I will not go into *all* the passages that referred to this particular prophecy. I will just tell you that there are a lot!

Do you remember Jesus telling His disciples to go to the town ahead of Him in order to find a donkey and bring it to Him (Matthew 21:2)? The Bible says little if anything else about it! The disciples found it just as Jesus had said. But whose donkey was it? Did the owner of the donkey read the Scriptures? Did He know the Messiah was coming? Was He hoping the Messiah would use his donkey? Were there multiple Jewish men raising donkeys like the lottery just hoping the Messiah would choose their donkey to ride on as the day drew near? Again, the Scripture does not say. It does say that the people laid down their cloaks and branches for Him, making a royal path for His donkey to walk on. And the Messiah fulfilled a prophecy right before their eyes.

Jesus is still fulfilling prophecy today. He did not stop fulfilling prophecy when He rose from the dead. Many prophecies about the end times and about Jesus returning again have yet to be fulfilled. Some are being fulfilled before *our* very eyes...*if*, we pay attention. Jesus still has things to do in the world and in your life. He is still the King of Kings and Lord of Lords. Look for Him this Christmas.

Thanks for reading! Want more free devotionals and resources?

Visit beccaharbert.com for more

Follow Becca's Facebook page:
Becca Harbert, Author for more free resources.

Kids' songs and parenting videos on Becca Harbert,
Author's YouTube channel.

Want Becca to speak at your Moms Group? Or Church?
Email growingtruegold@gmail.com.

Want Becca's kids' book *The Nut Donut* that teaches children how to live out their faith by listening to the Holy Spirit. Scan the QR code below.

BexBooks points people to Christ
through resources that explain the Bible.